YES I HAVE SPENDING PROBLEMS D|

Copyright © 2022 by Yes I Have Anxiety, Inc.

All rights reserved.

Thank you for purchasing an authorized edition of this book and for complying with copyright laws by not reproducing, scanning, or distributing any part of it in any form without permission.

Consumer Use Disclaimer: The "Yes I Have" book series was created in light-hearted, relatable fun to create distractions from things individuals may be dealing with. All "Yes I Have" books are not intended to diagnose medical conditions nor provide a cure for any medical conditions. This book is not meant to be a replacement for real medical intervention if needed.

ISBN: 978-1-958083-18-5

First Edition: April 2022

Yes I Have Anxiety, Inc.
Grove, Ok 74345

WHAT ARE YOU DEALING WITH?
WE GOT YOU!

Visit www.YesIHave.com for more books!

Do you have an idea for the next "Yes I Have®" book? Reach out to us through our website!

You might just see your idea in a future book!

What are you dealing with?

YES I HAVE® _____

Draw Some Money Out of The Window Since That is Where You are Throwing it.

WEEKLY *Budget*

Income

Source of Income	Amount
Total	

Expenses

Bills & Utilities		Groceries & Eating Out		Car & Transportation	
	$		$		$
	$		$		$
	$		$		$
	$		$		$
	$		$		$
	$		$		$
	$		$		$
	$		$		$
Total		Total		Total	
Shopping		Entertainment		Miscellaneous	
	$		$		$
	$		$		$
	$		$		$
	$		$		$
	$		$		$
	$		$		$
	$		$		$
	$		$		$
Total		Total		Total	

Total Expenses	

Savings

Goal:		Actual:	

Put Dollar Signs All Over This Page.

Cut up the Credit Cards.

Let's Pretend You are Rich.

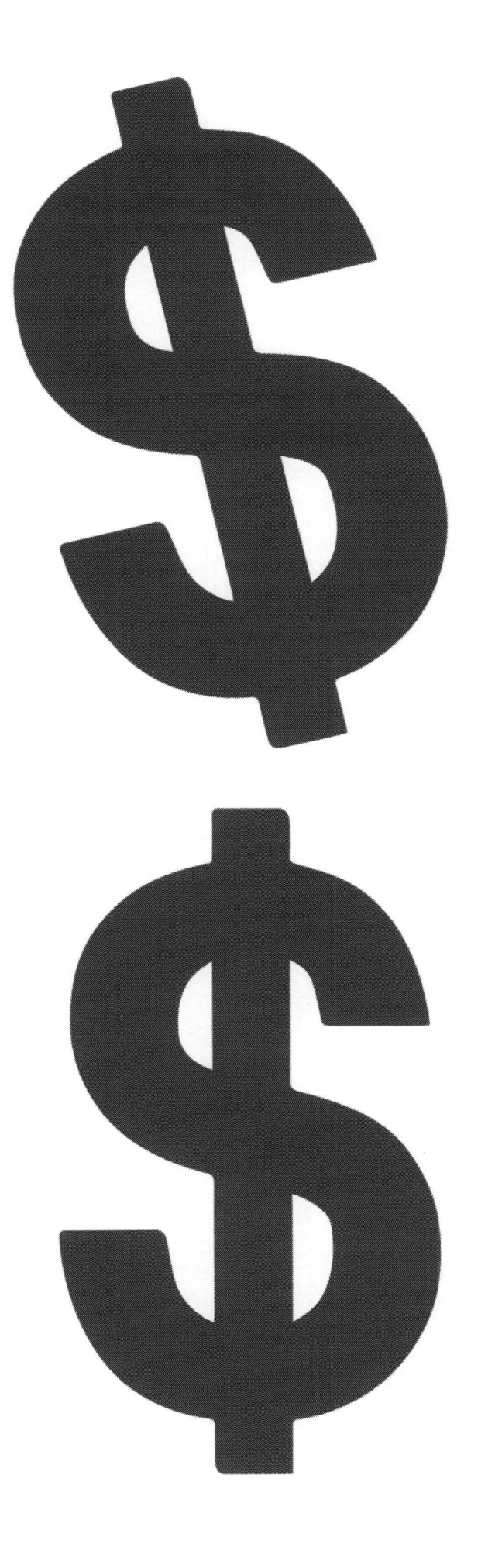

Add Bling to the
Dollar Signs.

Use This Page to Calculate How Much You Have Spent on Fast Food/Eating Out This Month.

Find the Counterfeit!

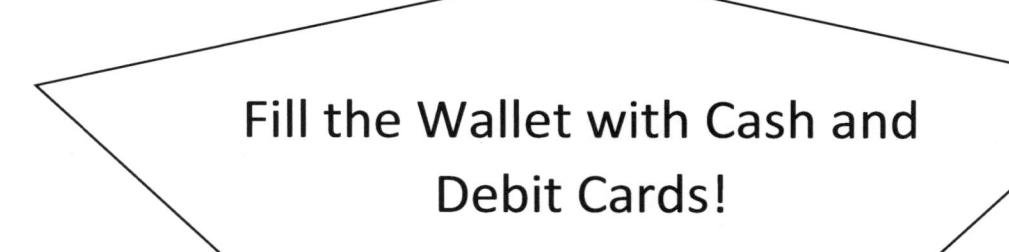

Fill the Wallet with Cash and Debit Cards!

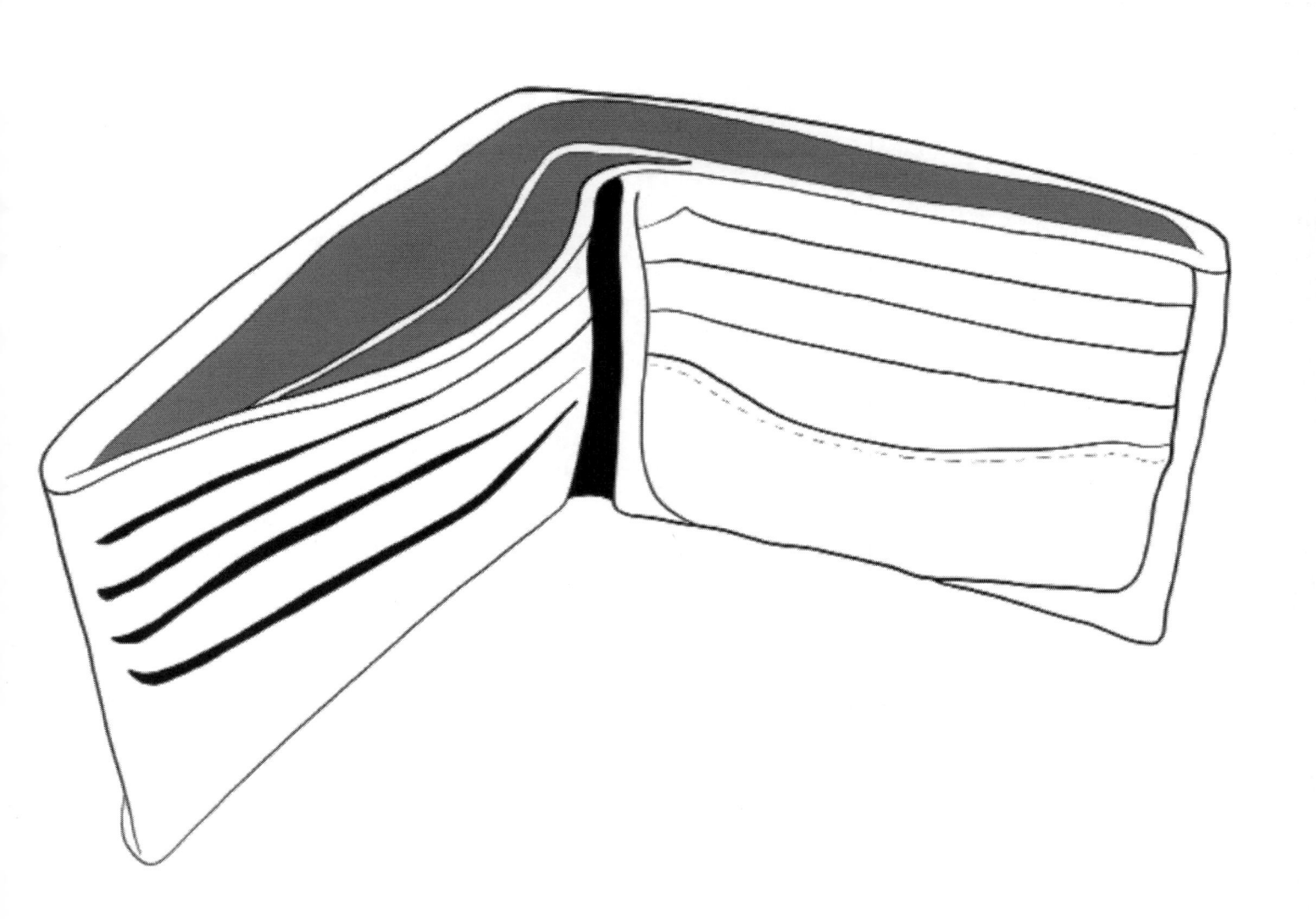

#BROKEFOLK

#BROKEFOLK

#BROKEFOLK

#BROKEFOLK

#BROKEFOLK

#JustColorIt

Write Yourself a BIG Check.

1025

DATE

PAY TO THE
ORDER OF

$

DOLLARS

Security Features
Included
Details on Back

MEMO

⑈000000000⑈ ⑈000000000⑈ 1025

How Would You Spend it?

Cover This Page in Ice Cubes
to Freeze Your Bank Account!

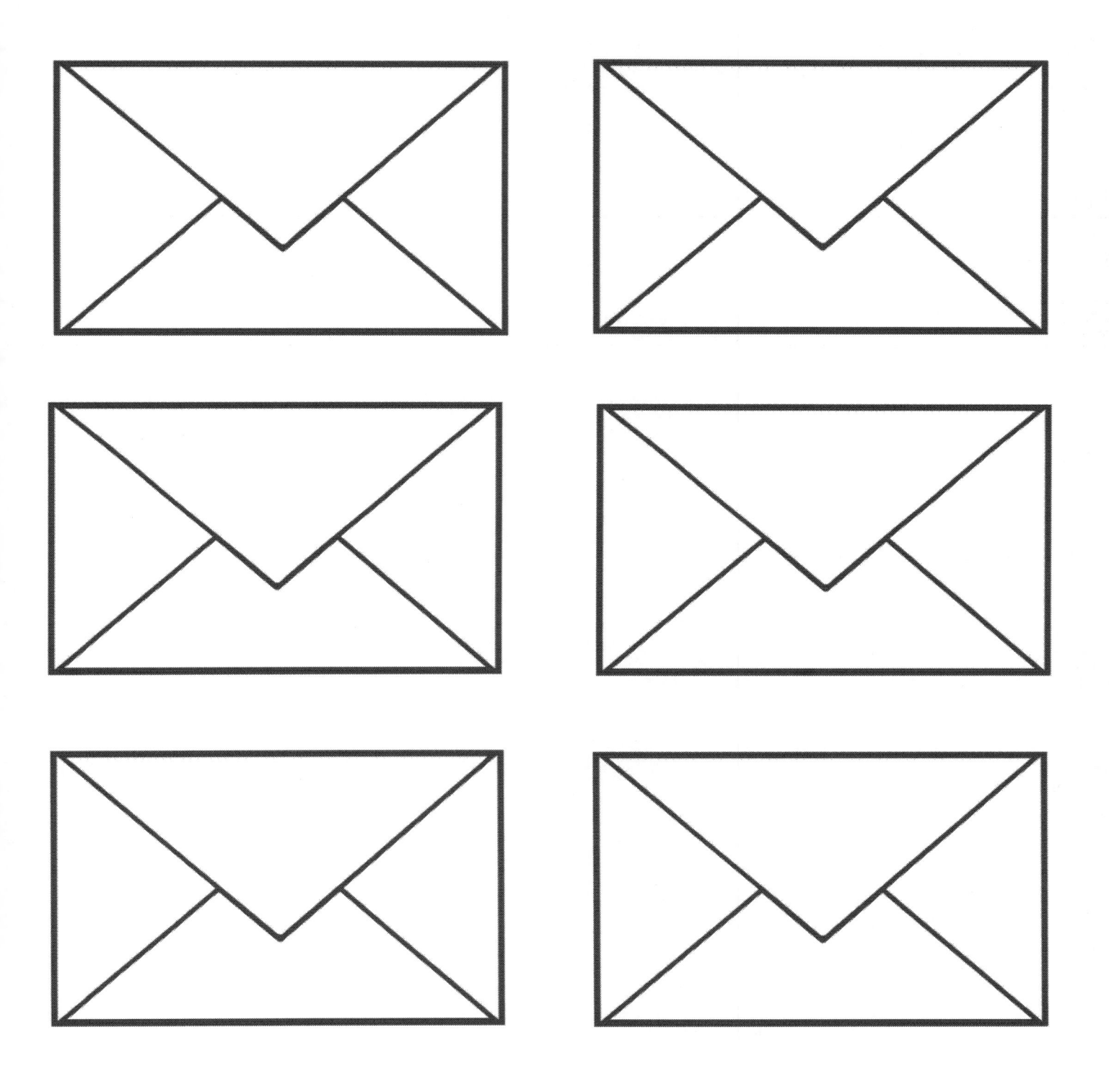

Fix the Hole You Burnt in
Your Pocket.

Use The Table Below to Cost Compare Different Grocery Stores in Your Area.			
Eggs			
Milk			
Bread			
Ground Meat			
Cheese			
Bananas			
Ice Cream			

Make This a Winning Lottery Ticket.

$5 WIN UP TO 15 TIMES!

TAX FREE $500,000!
YESICAN LOTTERY

MYSTERY BONUS   MYSTERY BONUS   MYSTERY BONUS

UNCOVER A $10, $20, $50, OR $100 PRIZE SYMBOL
in any of the MYSTERY BONUS spots, win that prize instantly.

WINNING NUMBERS

YOUR NUMBERS

TAX FREE PRIZES OF $500,000

Match any of YOUR NUMBERS to any of the WINNING NUMBERS,
win prize shown before that number. Get a STAR, win that prize
automatically, Get a HEART, win all 12 PRIZES shown.

Fill Your Shopping Basket with Groceries.

Put Your Face on the Money!

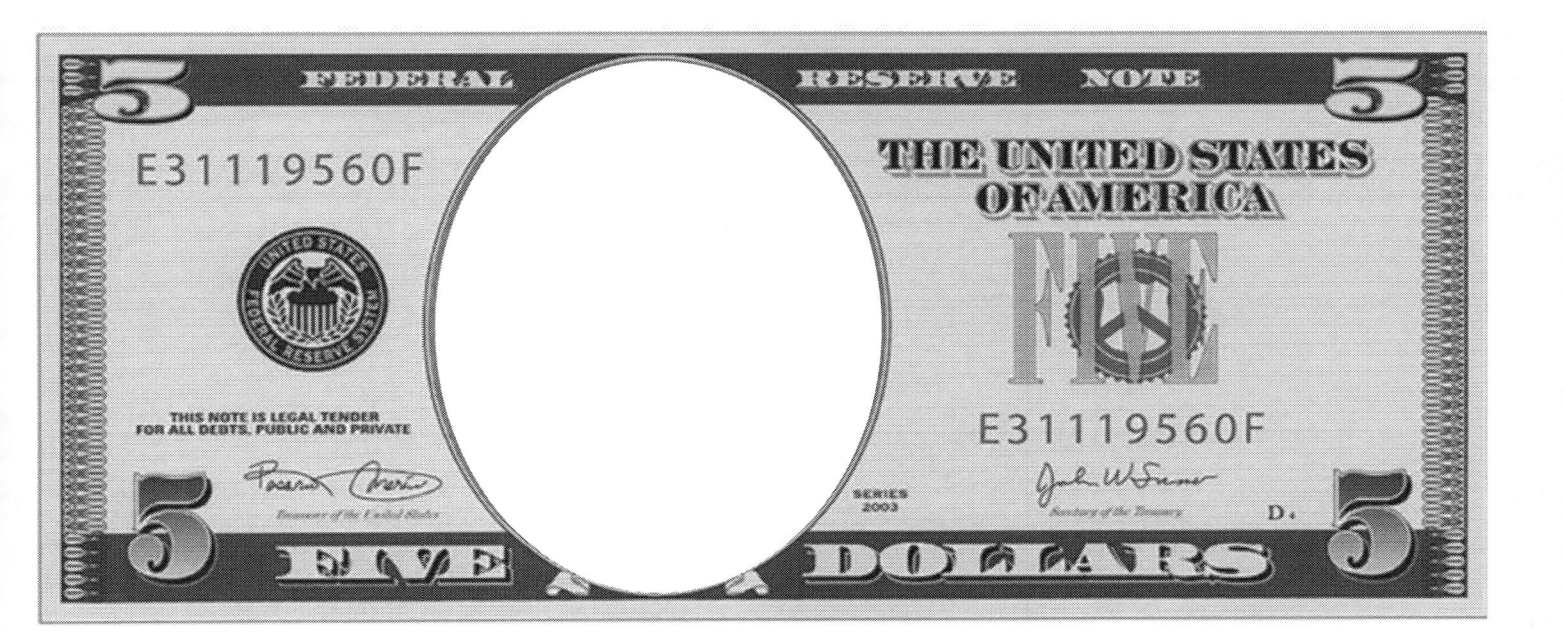

You're Having a Garage Sale to Earn Some Extra Cash! Price Your Items!

What Fast Food Restaurant is Your Weakness?

Cut out These Coupons.
We Know You Need Them.

How Many Words Can You Make From "I'M BROKE"?

_____   _____

_____   _____

_____   _____

_____   _____

_____   _____

_____   _____

_____   _____

_____   _____

Who Says Money Doesn't
Grow on Trees?
Decorate Your Money Tree!

Change "DECLINED" to "APPROVED".

Fill the Pot with Gold.

CREDIT SCORE

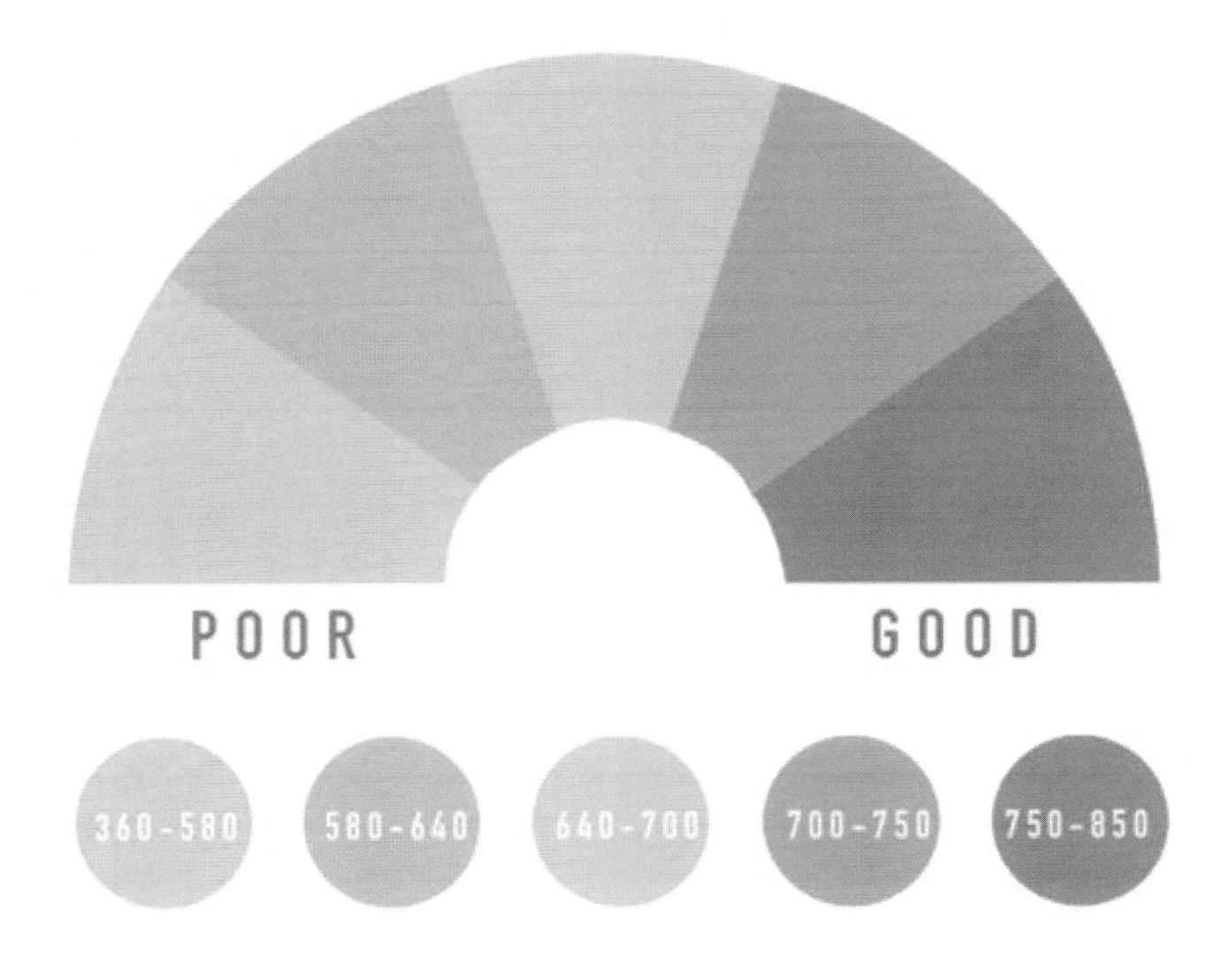

POOR   GOOD

360-580   580-640   640-700   700-750   750-850

Draw a Meter Where Your
Credit Score is at.

Write the Total Amount of Money at the End of Each Row.

Make This Purse a Designer Purse.

What do You Wish Gas Prices Were Right Now?

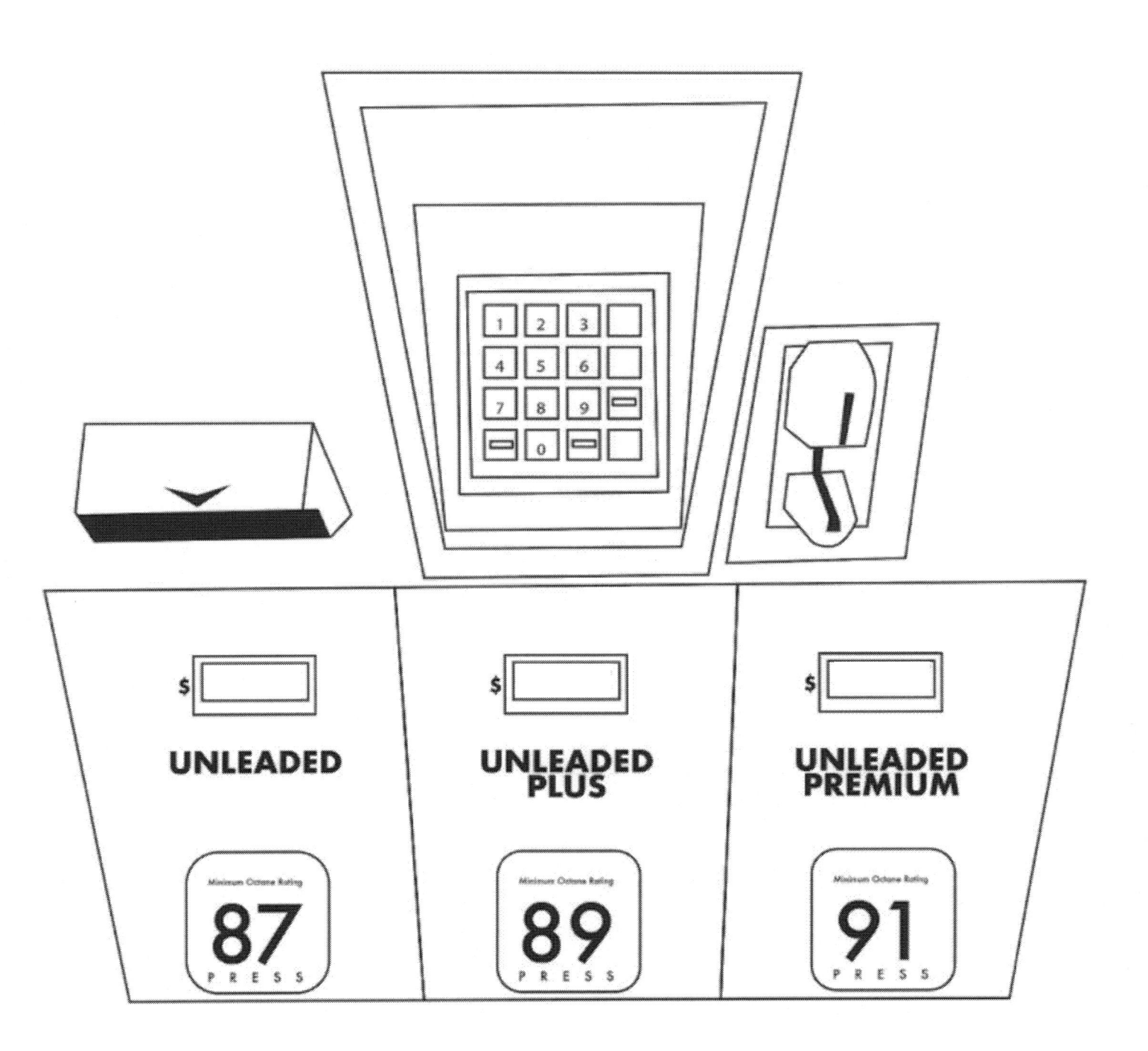

Make This Small House into the Bigger House That You Deserve!

You Lost Your Wallet! Find it.

Let's See Those Budget At-Home Nails!

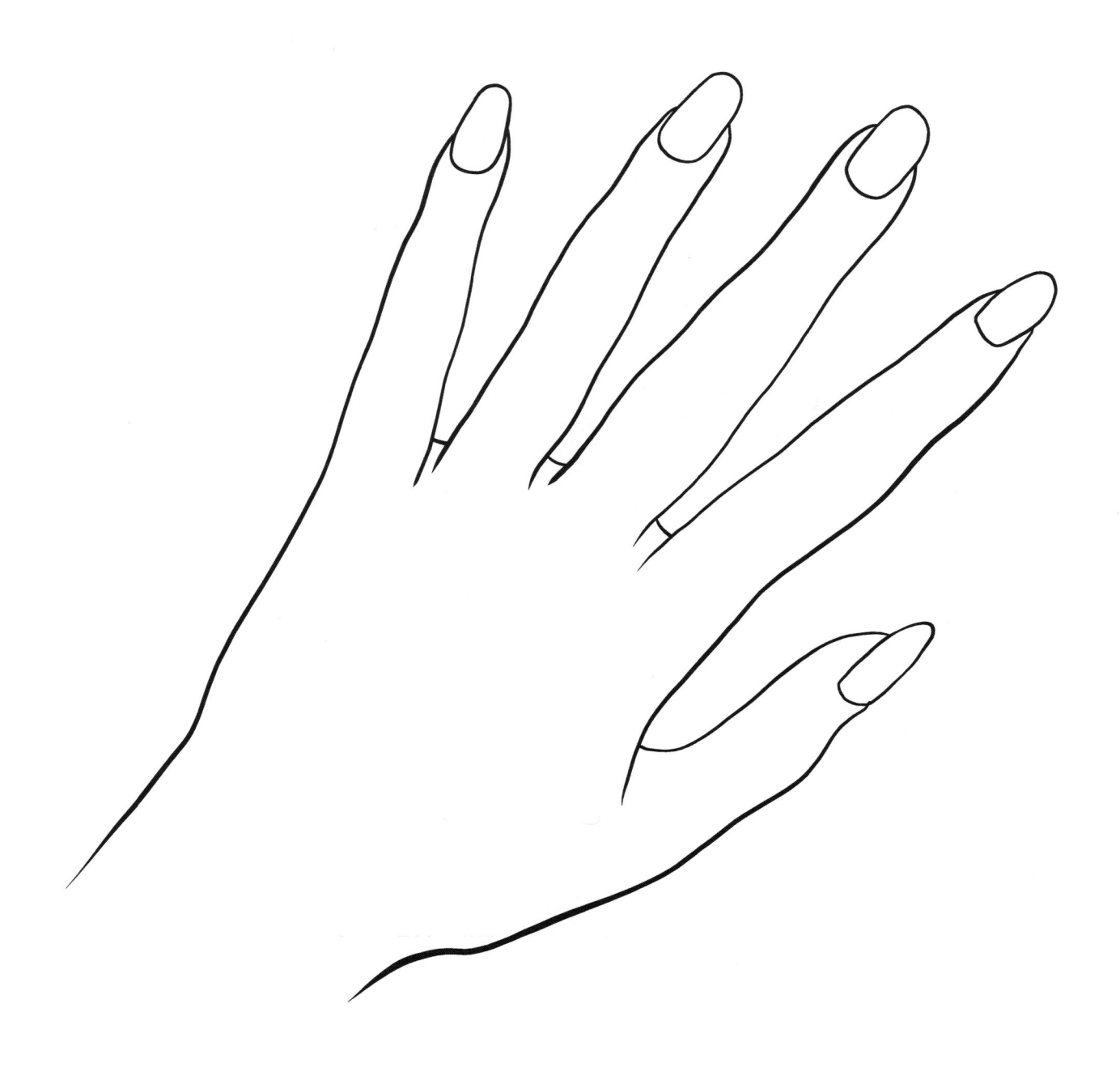

Add Zeros to the One Dollar Bills to Make Them 100 Dollar Bills.

Recipe

prep time   cook time   serves

INGREDIENTS   DIRECTIONS

Recipe

prep time   cook time   serves

INGREDIENTS   DIRECTIONS

Disguise Your Money Bags so They Don't Get Stolen!

Where are Your Favorite
Places to Shop?!

Search Around Your House and Try to Find the Oldest Penny You Can Find. What Year is it from?

Get Your Online Shopping Packages off the Front Porch.

YES I HAVE

Your personal checking account statement

From March 12, 2004 to April 12, 2004

RBCPDA0001-123456789-01-000001-1-0001   19715

SUSAN SAMPLE
1234 ANY STREET, SUITE 5678
ADDRESS LINE #2
CITY, PROVINCE A1B 2C3

Your account number: 02782-5094431

Deal. With. It.

Summary of your account for this period

Signature Plus 02782-5094431

Your opening balance on March 12, 2004	$4,247.14
Total deposits into your account	+ 145.15
Total withdrawals from your account	- 727.50
Your closing balance on April 12, 2004	**= $3,664.79**

> ### YES I HAVE
>
> *Dear Susan, we're pleased to introduce you to digital imaging. Now you can retrieve images of cheques in seconds and view them online. It's as easy as a click of a mouse.*
>
> *Try our new digital imaging service today.*

Details of your account activity

Date	Description	Withdrawals ($)	Deposits ($)	Balance ($)
	Opening balance			4,247.14
15 Mar	Transfer		85.00	
	Interest paid		.15	
	ATM withdrawal	100.00		
	Interac purchase -1361 - Nasr Foods Inc.	47.82		4,184.47
17 Mar	Overdraft interest	0.93		4,183.54
18 Mar	Cheque #30	40.00		
	Cheque #31	148.11		3,995.43
19 Mar	ATM withdrawal	60.00		3,935.43
22 Mar	ATM withdrawal	20.00		
	Interac purchase - 1361 - The Bay	125.13		
	Interac purchase - 1361 - Highland Farms	6.94		3,783.36

Change Your Withdrawals to Deposits!

Write a List of all Your Subscriptions.

Noodle Soup

What is Your Favorite
Noodle Soup Flavor?

$75.00	$15.00	$7.79	$699.99
$205.00	$23.99	$1005.99	$8.13
$480.85	$65.00	$500.00	$8.99
$13.00	$100.00	$30.50	$3.26
$48.00	$99.97	$88.20	$59.99

Cross Out the Prices and Put Them on Sale!

Paint the Piggy Bank!

Color Your Shoe Collection!

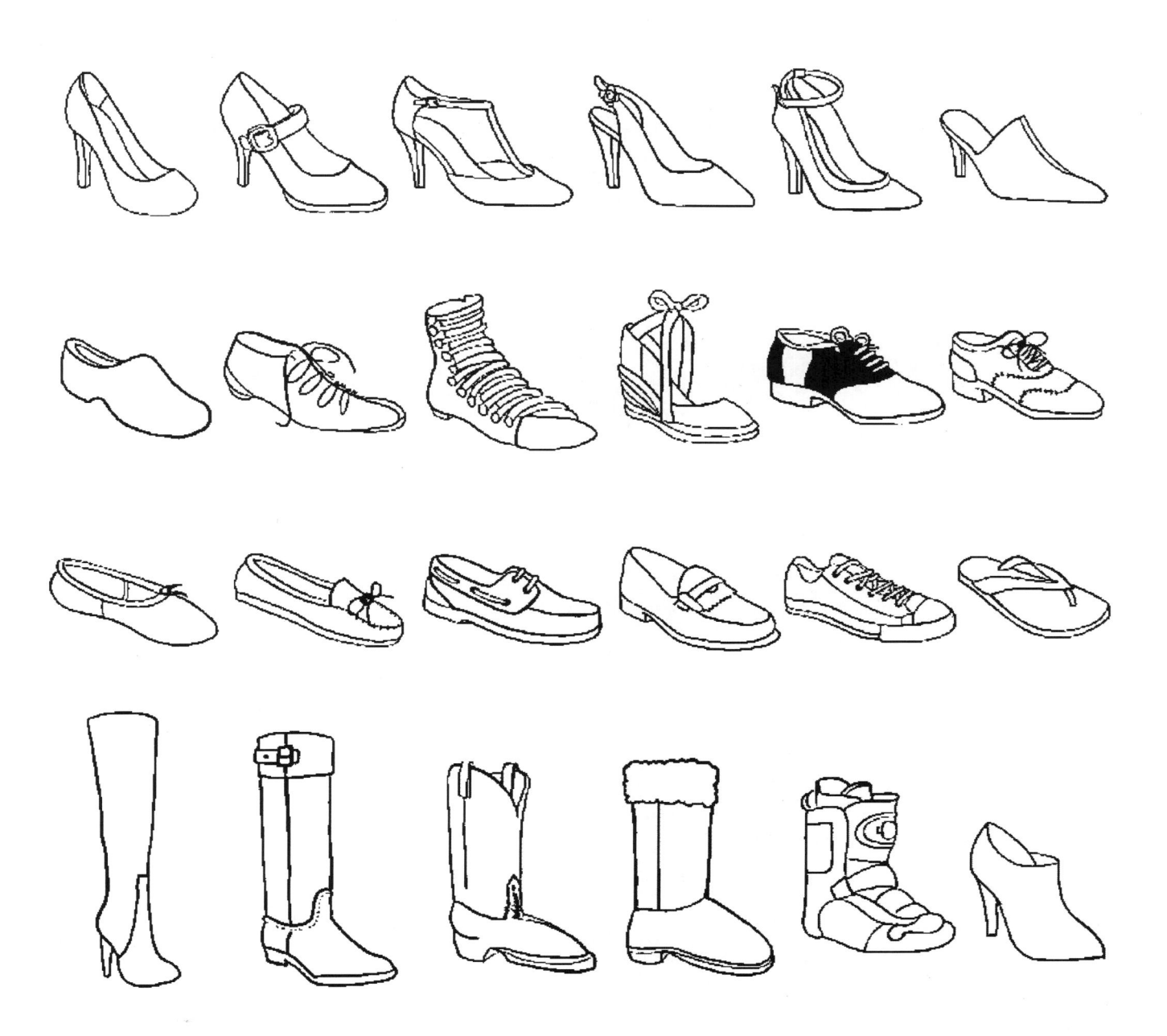

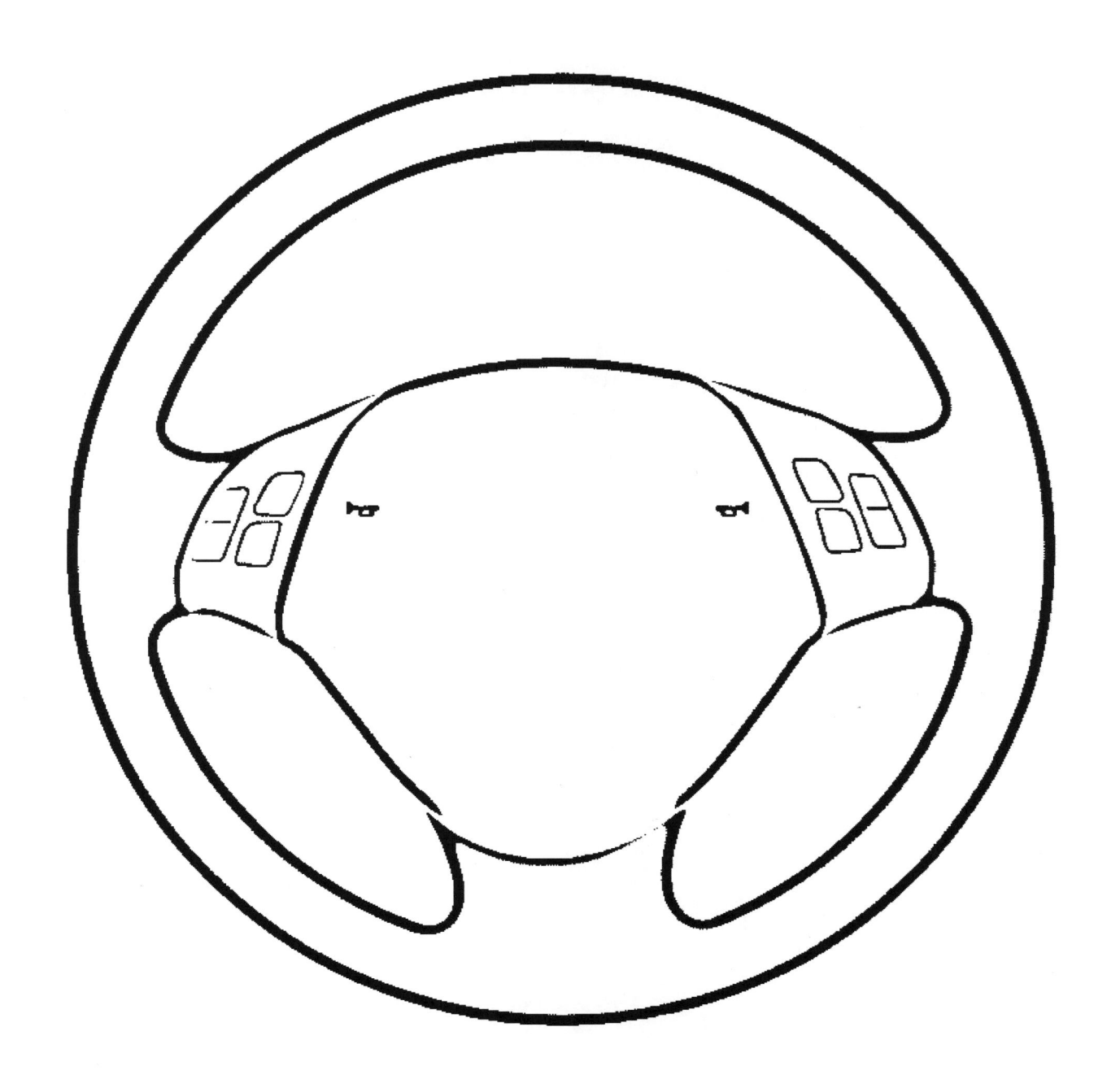

What Make of Car Do You
Wish to Drive?

CASH RECEIPT
#5225523

Thursday 05/04/18 16.33 PM

ITEM DESCRIPTION	QTY	PRICE
Aliquam molestie	1	$ 9.99
Auctor vitae	1	$ 5.20

Your Business Name		SUBTOTAL	$ 15.19
The Brown Street 3		TAX	$ 1.30
54322		DISCOUNT	$ 15%
State Adress, Country		TOTAL	$ 14.02
422 634 764			

THANK YOU FOR CHOOSING US!

ORDER RECEIPT
#676432

The Brown Street 3	Friday
54322	02/01/18
State Adress, Country	17.13 PM
422 634 764	

DESCRIPTION	PRICE
Aliquam molestie	$ 9.99
Auctor vitae	$ 5.20
Pharetr	$ 3.85
Semper	$ 8.30
Lorem	$ 5.30
Ipsum	$ 2.60

ORDER TOTAL	$ 35.24

Transaction Id	#644352
Transaction Type	Mastercard
Card Id	xxx xxx xxx 3333
Response	Approved
Approval Code	15543

FOR INFORMATION ON PRODUCT GUARANTEES VISIT
WWW.YOURWEBSITE.COM

RECEIPT

#5225523
Thursday 05/04/18 16.33 PM

ITEM DESCRIPTION	QTY	PRICE
Aliquam molestie	1	$ 9.99
Auctor vitae	1	$ 5.20
Aliquam molestie	1	$ 9.99
Auctor vitae	1	$ 5.20
Aliquam molestie	1	$ 9.99
Auctor vitae	1	$ 5.20
Aliquam molestie	1	$ 9.99
Auctor vitae	1	$ 5.20

Your Business Name		SUBTOTAL	$ 15.19
The Brown Street 3		TAX	$ 1.30
54322		DISCOUNT	$ 15%
State Adress, Country		TOTAL	$ 14.02
422 634 764			

THANK YOU FOR CHOOSING US!

SHOP NAME

The Brown Street 3	Friday
54322	02/01/18
State Adress, Country	17.13 PM
422 634 764	

ORDER RECEIPT #531

ITEM NO.	ITEM DESCRIPTION	QTY	PRICE
#142	Dipiscing	1	$ 15.99
#86	Aliquam molestie	1	$ 9.99
#63	Auctor vitae	1	$ 5.20
#394	Pharetr	1	$ 3.85
#41	Semper	1	$ 8.30

	SUBTOTAL	$ 43.33
	TAX	$ 4.30
	TOTAL	$ 46.63

Transaction Id	#24521
Transaction Type	Mastercard
Card Id	xxx xxx xxx 1111
Response	Approved
Approval Code	295235

THANK YOU FOR CHOOSING US!

CASH RECEIPT
#1111111

The Brown Street 3	Friday
54322	02/01/18
State Adress, Country	17.13 PM
422 634 764	

ITEM NO.	ITEM DESCRIPTION	QTY	PRICE
#142	Dipiscing	1	$ 15.99
#86	Aliquam molestie	1	$ 9.99
#63	Auctor vitae	1	$ 5.20

	TOTAL	$ 31.18

THANK YOU FOR SHOPPING WITH US!

Tear Out the Receipts to Get Rid of the Evidence!

Pimp the Ride.

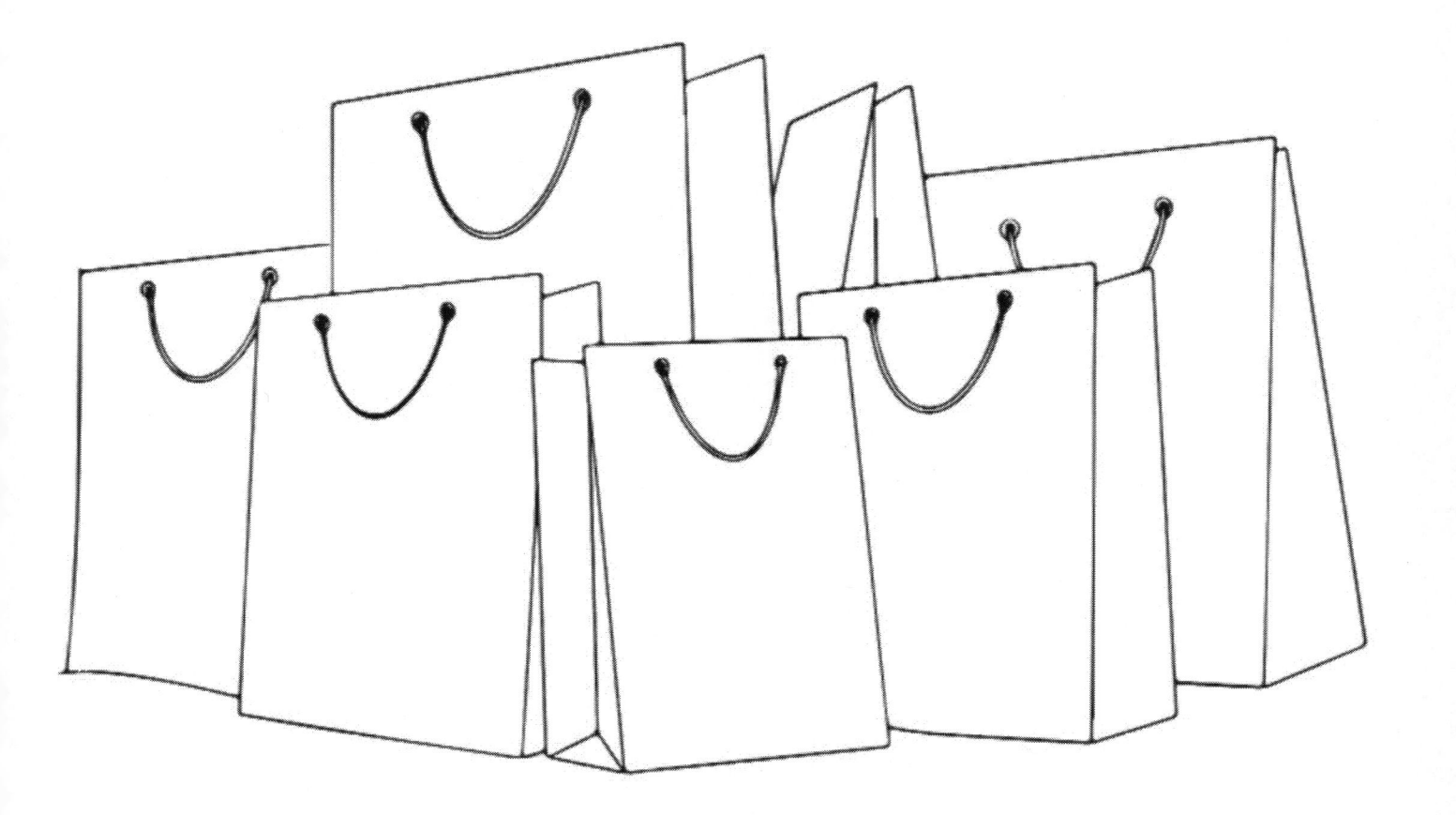

Where Would You Go Shopping if You Could Afford it?

Cover the Shovel in Mud
Because You Used it to Dig
Yourself Out of Debt.

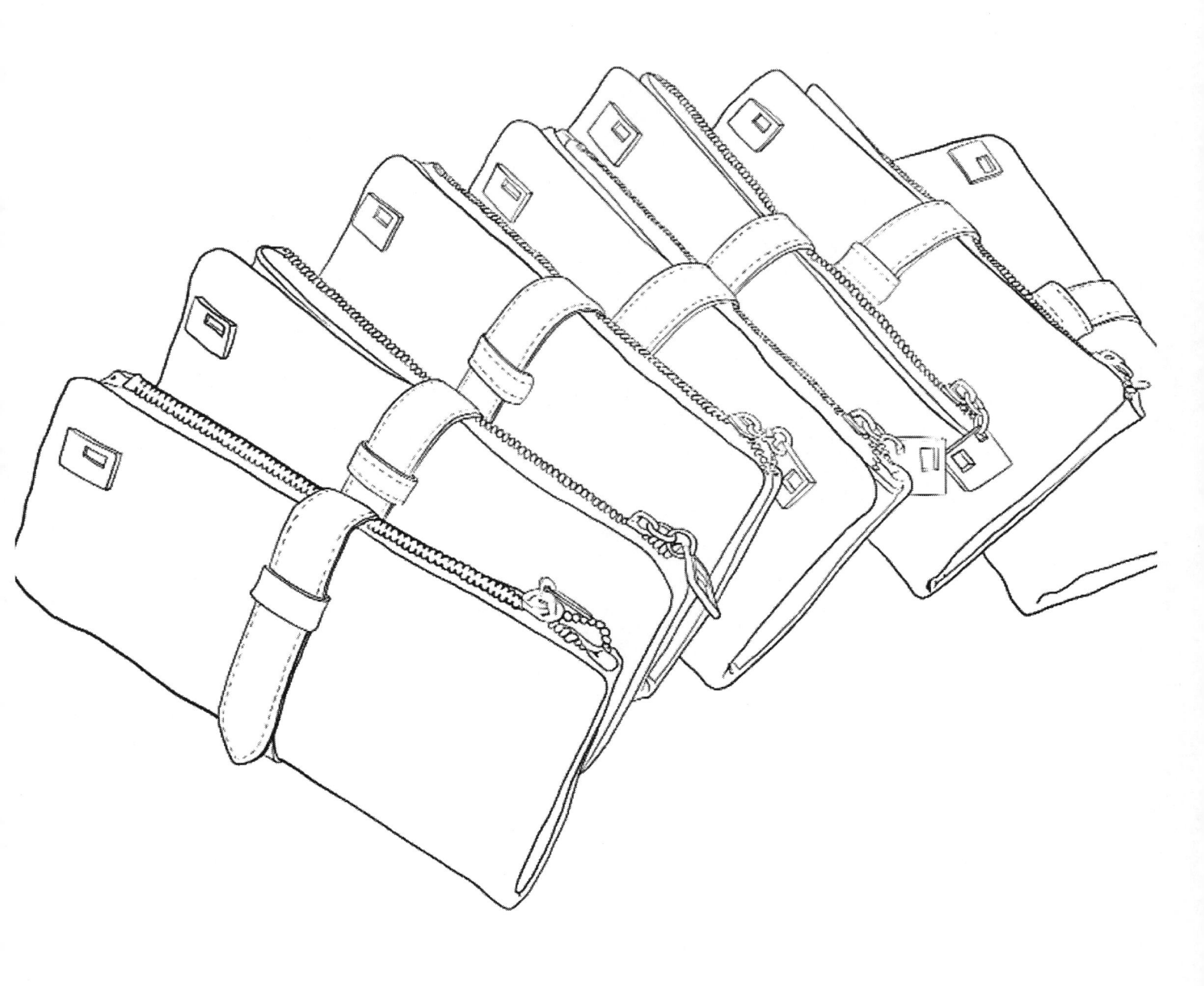

Design a Wallet Collection!

Don't miss out on <u>FREE books</u> and New Book Announcements!!!

Follow us on our social media platforms to be included in weekly giveaways, book tour location announcements, new book releases, and videos for page idea inspiration!!!

officialyesihave

yesihaveofficial

Yes I Have Books

Yes I Have Official

JOIN OUR NEWSLETTER!:
Text
YESIHAVE
TO 22828 to get started!

Hey Fans!! If you post your page videos on social media and one goes viral, we want to know! Send your video to us at yesihavebooks@gmail.com

We showcase our viral fan videos on our website and social media outlets! We have 100+ viral videos and counting!

Want to Find More Books?

Scan the QR Code, Then Decorate it!

Scan Me

MOOD SWINGS PERFECTIONISM
KIDS ANXIETY STRESS IDEAS
HARD TIMES PETS BOREDOM
BABY FEVER CHRISTMAS FEVER

Made in the USA
Las Vegas, NV
28 October 2022

58311852R00061